101
Gourmet
Cookies

for EVERYONE

Text © 2010 by Wendy L. Paul
Photographs © 2010 by Marielle Hayes

ISBN: 978-1-59955-409-9

Published by Bonneville Books, an imprint of Cedar Fort, Inc., 2373 W. 700 S., Springville, UT 84663
Distributed by Cedar Fort, Inc., www.cedarfort.com

LIBRARY OF CONGRESS CATALOGING-IN-PUBLICATION DATA
    Paul, Wendy.
      101 gourmet cookies for everyone / Wendy Paul.
      p. cm.
      ISBN 978-1-59955-409-9
      1. Cookies. I. Title.
      TX772.P325 2010
      641.8'654--dc22

      2010012526

Cover and page design by Angela D. Olsen
Cover design © 2010 by Lyle Mortimer
Edited by Kimiko M. Hammari
Printed in China
10 9 8 7 6 5 4 3 2 1
Printed on acid-free paper

It's what's on the INSIDE that counts

101 Gourmet Cookies

for EVERYONE

There's always a reason to bake with

WENDY PAUL

BONNEVILLE BOOKS
SPRINGVILLE, UTAH

Dedication

· ·

*This cookbook is dedicated to my husband, Brian,
who endures my constant desire to make new recipes,
tastes them, gives me good criticism, and loves me
even when I spend all my free time
in the kitchen. I love you!*

Cindy,
there's always
a reason to
bake! Wendy Paul

Contents

Everyone loves a good cookie...

Cookies can be classic. They can also be a work of art or a way of celebrating. Cookies are great to eat anytime, anywhere, especially when there is a cookie for everyone!

Yes, I still love spending time in the kitchen. I have been making the cookie recipes you love and cherish easy, fast, and foolproof. Only the best of the best made this cookbook, and I personally made each and every recipe at least once.

Over the last 18 months, the most frequently asked question was, "Is there a cookie for me?" I have met many people who face food challenges each day. These challenges include food allergies, medical problems, or a chosen food lifestyle. This cookbook covers a little bit of everything, while not compromising on the taste or texture.

From Forgetting the Calories, to Watching Your Waistline, to Gluten-Free and Flavorful, and last, but certainly not least, Surprisingly Vegan, there truly is a cookie that not only tastes great but looks great too. A cookie for everyone!

Go ahead, get your grocery list ready, and take a trip to the store. Find your favorite cookie recipe and start baking! Your family and friends will thank you for the wonderful home baked creation.

Happy Baking!

—Wendy L. Paul

Tips for Success

To make any cookie bake better, without losing substance, refrigerate the cookie dough for 1 hour, covered. This chills the dough just enough so the cookies won't flatten out when baked.

Use a cookie scoop to measure out the cookie dough. The scoop makes each cookie even in size, which makes baking times uniform. A cookie scoop is one of my favorite baking tools.

Tips for soft, chewy cookies: Do not overmix the dough or use too much flour. Bake cookies the minimum amount of time, even though the center may look slightly underbaked. Let cookies stand on baking sheet for one to three minutes to continue to bake. Then remove to cooling rack.

Most cookie dough freezes well up to three months. Thaw dough in the refrigerator until it's soft enough to use. Then follow the recipe directions for baking.

To have future batches of cookies ready in minutes, measure out dough for each cookie and drop dough onto cookie sheets; freeze until firm. When frozen, remove dough from cookie sheets, place in heavy-duty freezer bags, and freeze until you want to bake a batch of cookies. Then thaw the cookie dough and follow recipe directions for baking.

To fix dry or crumbled cookie dough, add 1–2 Tbsp. milk or cream. Knead into the dough, rather than mixing with your beaters.

If your dough is sticking while rolling out, use a pastry cloth to make rolling the dough easier and to help prevent dough from sticking. Rub flour evenly onto rolling pin cover and pastry cloth for easy handling. Or, if dough appears to be too soft, refrigerate for about one hour.

Wondering how to tell if your cookie is done baking?
Here are some helpful hints:

If the recipe calls for 7–10 minutes of baking time, set your timer for 7 minutes. Then check your cookies every minute after that until the edges are lightly golden. Any darker than that and your cookie will be very crispy and possibly overdone. Cookies can go from underdone to done in less than one minute. Watch the first batch carefully so you know what your oven and cookie recipe need.

Forget the Calories

Cookies

Citrus Crinkles
Browned Butter Crinkles
 with Browned Butter Frosting
Chocolate Orange Crinkles
Spectacular Snickerdoodles
Peanut Butter Goodness
Almond Jelly Thumbprints
White Chocolate Gems
Grandma Y's German Cookies
Rosemary & Lavender Shortbread
 with a Lavender Glaze
Basil & Lemon Shortbread
 with a Lemon Glaze
Chocolate Chip Pudding Cookies
Soft Sour Cream Sugar
 Cookies *with a Vanilla*
 Buttercream Frosting

Root Beer Float Cookies
 with a Cream Glaze
Piña Colada Cookies
 with a Coconut Glaze
Make Some Whoopie Pies
Cherry Chocolate Cookies
Grandma Lu's Persimmon Cookies
Almond Wedding Cookies
Mini Peanut Butter Bites
Amish Cookies
Oatmeal Butterscotch Cookies
Julia's Molasses Cookies
Sunny Lemonade Cookies
Cowboy Up
Double Chocolate Chip Cookies

Bars

Creamy Lemon Blueberry Delight
Luscious Lemon Bars
Key Lime Surprise
Heavenly Almond Bars
Magically Delicious
Crazy for Cranberries
  with a Cream Cheese Frosting
  and White Chocolate Drizzle
Melt in Your Mouth Maple Bars
Southern Sweet Potato Bars
  with Maple Glaze
Caramel Apple Bars
Best of All Pumpkin Bars
Perfectly Peanut Butter Bars
Christmas Cherry Bars
Traditional Nanaimo Bars
Coconut Pecan Pie Bars

Brownies

Triple Chocolate Fudge Brownies
Black Forest Brownies
  with Cherry Pie Filling Drizzle
Better to Be Blonde
Chocolate Caramel Brownies
Peanut Butter Cup Brownies
Give Me S'more Brownies
Sinful Chocolate Raspberry
  Brownies *with a Raspberry Glaze*
Little Turtles
Mint Patty Brownies
Mayan Fudge Brownies
Nutty Bunch Brownies
Dreamy Creamy Brownies
There's Zucchini in here?
Candy Cane Brownies
Chocolate Pumpkin Brownies

Citrus Crinkles

Citrus buttery cookies that are great for any bake sale, brunch, or family gathering.
Only the crumbs will be left on this plate.

2 sticks butter, softened

1 cup sugar

3 egg yolks

2 Tbsp. lemon zest

2 Tbsp. orange zest

pinch of salt

1½ tsp. soda

1½ tsp. lemon extract

2½ cups flour

3 Tbsp. orange marmalade, melted

1–2 Tbsp. lemonade concentrate, melted

Cream butter and sugar together. Add egg yolks, lemon and orange zest, and salt. Add soda and lemon extract. Fold in flour. Stir until combined. Form balls the size of walnuts. Chill dough balls for 1 hour in the refrigerator. Bake at 350 degrees for 8–10 minutes or until cookies are lightly golden.

In the meantime, melt marmalade and lemonade concentrate together over medium heat.

Remove cookies from oven. Brush with melted marmalade and lemonade concentrate. Cool completely.

Browned Butter Crinkles
with Browned Butter Frosting

Browned Butter Crinkles

This recipe was inspired by my friend Darin on KSL's Studio 5. After appearing on the show, I asked him what his favorite cookie is. This browned butter crinkle is the result of my inspiration from him. Darin, I hope you enjoy this one as much as my thighs have. You simply can't eat just one. P.S. The cookie is just as good as the frosting!

2 sticks butter, softened

1 cup sugar

3 egg yolks

pinch of salt

1½ tsp. baking soda

1½ tsp. vanilla

2⅓ cups flour

Browned Butter Frosting

Beat butter and sugar together. Add egg yolks and salt, and then add soda and vanilla. Fold in flour. Stir until combined. Form balls the size of walnuts. Chill dough balls for 1 hour in the refrigerator. Dip tops in sugar. Press flat with the bottom of a glass and place on an ungreased cookie sheet. Bake at 350 degrees for 8–10 minutes or until lightly golden. Remove from oven and let the cookies stand for 1 minute on the cookie sheet. Remove to a wire rack and cool completely. Frost.

1 stick butter

4 cups powdered sugar

1 tsp. vanilla

½ cup heavy cream or more for right consistency

I don't think there is much to say, but you MUST try it.

Browned Butter Frosting

In a small skillet, brown butter over medium heat until golden brown flecks appear. Butter will become a little foamy. Stir occasionally to make butter cook evenly. Remove from heat and cool slightly. Add powdered sugar, vanilla, and cream. Beat on medium high until a creamy texture to your liking forms. Spread onto cooled butter crinkles.

Chocolate Orange Crinkles

Orange and chocolate are a perfect pairing of flavors. Enjoy these rich little buttery cookies with orange zest and chocolate drizzled on top.

2 cups butter, softened

1 cup sugar

3 egg yolks

2 Tbsp. orange juice concentrate

1½ tsp. orange extract

2 Tbsp. grated orange zest

pinch of salt

1½ tsp. baking soda

2½ cups flour

¼ cup chocolate chips, melted

Beat butter and sugar together. Add egg yolks, orange concentrate, orange extract, orange zest, and salt. Then add soda. Fold in flour. Stir until combined.

Form balls the size of walnuts. Chill dough balls for 1 hour in the refrigerator. Dip tops in sugar. Press flat with a fork on an ungreased cookie sheet.

Bake at 350 degrees for 8–10 minutes until lightly golden. Remove from oven and cool completely. Drizzle melted chocolate over the tops of cooled cookies.

Spectacular Snickerdoodles

*This recipe is a family favorite. They are soft and chewy, just like a snickerdoodle should be.
My brother loves a good, soft snickerdoodle cookie.*

½ cup butter

1 cup sugar

1 egg

1 tsp. vanilla

½ tsp. baking soda

½ tsp. cream of tartar

2–2½ cups flour

½ tsp. cinnamon

4 Tbsp. sugar

Cream butter and sugar together until light and fluffy. Add egg, vanilla, baking soda, and cream of tartar. Gradually add flour and mix until combined.

Cover and chill 1 hour. Roll dough into 1-inch balls and dip into cinnamon and sugar mixture.

Place on lightly greased cookie sheet and bake at 375 degrees for 8–10 minutes, or until edges are lightly golden. Remove from oven and cool completely.

Peanut Butter Goodness

Peanut Butter Goodness

This recipe is for my friend Reagan. She loves peanut butter so much! The only thing better than the smell of fresh baked cookies is the taste. Maybe it's sneaking a taste of the batter as you prepare them.

1 cup shortening

1 cup sugar

1 cup brown sugar

1 cup chunky peanut butter

2 eggs

2 tsp. baking soda

2¾ cups flour

Cream together shortening, sugars, and peanut butter. Add eggs and then flour and baking soda. Mix until combined.

Shape dough into logs and wrap in wax paper. Seal in airtight bag and chill or freeze for later. Slice cookies into ¼-inch slices.

Bake at 375 degrees for 8–10 minutes on an ungreased cookie sheet. Do not overbake. Remove from oven and cool completely.

Almond Jelly Thumbprints

Almond Jelly Thumbprints

These cookies have been a classic staple since the early 1940s. This is my version. Easy, simple, and full of flavor.

1½ cups butter, softened

1 cup sugar

1½ cups ground almonds

1 tsp. vanilla

pinch of salt

2¾–3 cups flour

1 cup raspberry or strawberry preserves

Cream together butter and sugar. Add ground almonds, vanilla, salt, and flour. Stir until combined.

Cover and refrigerate dough for 1 hour (IMPORTANT). Roll into 1-inch balls.

Place a thumbprint in the middle of each ball and bake on a parchment lined cookie sheet at 375 degrees for 10–12 minutes. Remove from oven and allow cookies to cool completely.

Place a small spoonful of preserves in the middle of the cookie. Dust with powdered sugar, if desired.

White Chocolate Gems

I love white chocolate. I also love the combination of sweet and salty. This adorable no-bake cookie is a perfect combination. Not to mention pretty too!

½ cup Craisins

½ cup chopped pistachios or pecans

½ cup crushed pretzels

½ cup dried apricots, diced

½ cup mini marshmallows (optional)

1 bag white chocolate chips

nonstick spray

muffin pan (or mini muffin pan for smaller cookies)

Spray muffin tin with nonstick spray. Fill first 5 ingredients evenly between all muffin spaces.

Gently melt white chocolate in the microwave, 30 seconds at a time, stirring in between (it should only take about 1½ minutes at the most).

Place 1–2 tablespoons melted chocolate over each mound of nut mixture. Softly hit pan against the counter to get out air bubbles that may have formed under chocolate. Set aside to allow chocolate to harden.

Once chocolate is hard, use a knife to remove cookies and place any leftovers in an airtight container for up to 2 weeks.

Grandma Y's German Cookies

Traditions are important. This recipe has been around long before I joined the Paul family.
This cookie is perfect for dunking. A tasty German treat!

8 eggs

2 pounds brown sugar

¼ lb. shelled almonds, chopped fine

¼ lb. citron, chopped fine

1 tsp. nutmeg

2 tsp. cinnamon

2 tsp. cloves

2 tsp. allspice

2 tsp. baking powder

1 tsp. salt

6 cups flour

Beat eggs together. Add sugar. Mix well and add chopped almonds, citron, spices, baking powder, and salt. Add flour to make the consistency of sugar cookies.

Refrigerate overnight. Roll ½-inch thick. Cut into circles or another desired shape. (Dip cookie cutter in flour before each use. It will keep each cut of dough clean.)

Bake at 350 degrees for 8–10 minutes or until light brown. If the cookies get hard, place cookies and a slice of bread or cut apple in a closed container and they will become soft.

Rosemary & Lavender Shortbread

Rosemary & Lavender Shortbread

These cookies are incredible. I have a fresh rosemary bush in my garden, and rosemary is a staple in the breads and rolls that I bake. Now I am using rosemary in this cookie too! These cookies will stay fresh for up to 1 week—if they last that long.

1½ cups butter, softened

⅔ cup sugar

2 Tbsp. fresh rosemary, chopped (or 3½ Tbsp. dried rosemary)

2¾ cups flour

pinch of salt

Lavender Glaze

Cream together butter and sugar until light and fluffy. Add rosemary, flour, and salt. Gently stir until combined.

Chill dough in refrigerator for 1 hour. On a floured surface, roll chilled dough to ⅓-inch. Cut out circles or rectangles, and place on a parchment lined baking sheet.

Bake at 375 degrees for 8–10 minutes or until lightly golden. Remove from oven and cool on a rack. Cover with lavender glaze while cookies are slightly warm.

2 cups powdered sugar

4–5 drops pure lavender essential oil

2 tsp. (or more) water

Lavender Glaze

Gently whisk all ingredients until all lumps are gone. Drizzle over rosemary cookies. Store cookies in an airtight container.

Basil & Lemon Shortbread

Basil & Lemon Shortbread

*After making the Rosemary & Lavender shortbread cookies, my brain started working overtime.
I can't just include one savory cookie, can I? This recipe came to life
and is satisfying and surprisingly scrumptious.*

1½ cups butter, softened

⅔ cup sugar

2 Tbsp. fresh basil, chopped
(or 3½ Tbsp. dried basil)

2 Tbsp. grated lemon zest,
divided

2¾ cups flour

pinch of salt

Lemon Glaze

Cream together butter and sugar until light and fluffy. Add basil, lemon zest, flour, and salt. Gently stir until combined.

Chill dough in refrigerator for 1 hour. On a floured surface, roll chilled dough to ⅓-inch. Cut out circles or rectangles, and place on a parchment lined baking sheet.

Bake at 375 degrees for 8–10 minutes or until lightly golden. Remove from oven and cool on a rack. Cover with lemon glaze while cookies are slightly warm.

---

2 cups powdered sugar

4–5 drops pure lemon essential
oil or lemon extract

2 tsp. (or more) water

Lemon Glaze

Gently whisk all ingredients together until all lumps are gone. Drizzle over cooled basil cookies. Store cookies in an airtight container.

Chocolate Chip Pudding Cookies

These cookies are by far the softest chocolate chip cookies I have ever tasted.
If they are still around tomorrow, they'll be even softer!

1 cup butter, softened

¼ cup sugar

¾ cup brown sugar

1 tsp. vanilla

2 eggs

1 (4-oz.) pkg. vanilla instant pudding mix (dry powder only)

1 tsp. baking soda

2¼ cups flour

2 cups semi-sweet chocolate chips

Cream together butter and sugars until light and fluffy. Add vanilla, eggs, and pudding mix.

In a separate bowl, mix together baking soda and flour and gently add to wet ingredients. Fold in chocolate chips. Use a small cookie scoop to drop dough onto lightly greased cookie sheet.

Bake at 350 degrees for 8–10 minutes, until sides become golden. Remove from oven and cool completely on a wire rack.

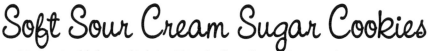

Soft Sour Cream Sugar Cookies

My sister is a fabulous cookie baker. This is her "special" recipe for extra-soft sour cream sugar cookies. They're like the kind you get from the store, only homemade. Thanks Heidi!

½ cup butter
½ cup sour cream
⅔ cup sugar
2 eggs
1 tsp. vanilla
3–3⅔ cups flour
1 tablespoon baking powder
½ tsp. baking soda
½ tsp. salt

Cream together butter, sour cream, and sugar. Add eggs and vanilla. In a separate bowl, combine flour, baking powder, baking soda, and salt. This dough will be slightly sticky.

Roll dough out on a lightly floured surface about ⅓-thick. Cut into desired shapes with cookie cutters. Bake at 425 degrees for 4–6 minutes. Remove cookies before they start to brown. Cool cookies completely before frosting with butter cream frosting.

Vanilla Buttercream Frosting

8 Tbsp. (1 stick) butter, room temperature
3¾ cups powdered sugar, sifted
3–4 Tbsp. milk (or cream)
2 tsp. vanilla

Place butter in a large mixing bowl. Beat until light and fluffy, about 30 seconds. Stop mixer before adding sugar to avoid a large mess. Add sugar, 3 tablespoons milk (or cream), and vanilla. Beat frosting, starting on slow, increasing your speed until frosting is nice and creamy. Add up to 1 more tablespoon milk (or cream) if frosting is too thick.

Root Beer Float Cookies

Root Beer Float Cookies

Life couldn't get much sweeter than a root beer float cookie.

¾ cup sugar

¾ cup brown sugar

1 cup butter, softened

¼ cup milk

2 eggs

2 Tbsp. root beer flavoring
   or extract

4 cups flour

pinch of salt

1 tsp. baking soda

Cream Glaze

Cream together sugars and butter until light and fluffy. Add milk, eggs, and root beer extract. Stir to combine. Add dry ingredients and mix until combined.

Roll dough into 1-inch balls. Refrigerate dough for 1 hour until firm. Then place on a lightly greased cookie sheet.

Bake at 350 degrees for 8–10 minutes. Remove from oven and cool completely. Frost with the cream glaze.

2–3 Tbsp. cream

1½ cups powdered sugar

½ tsp. vanilla

Cream Glaze

Gently whisk all ingredients until all lumps are gone. Drizzle or spread over cooled cookies.

Piña Colada Cookies

Piña Colada Cookies

Let's have a party! You bring the Piña Colada Cookies, and I'll make the drinks.

¾ cup sugar

½ cup butter

1 tsp. coconut extract

⅓ cup pineapple ice cream topping

2 eggs

2 cups flour

1 tsp. baking powder

1 tsp. baking soda

¾ cup flaked coconut

pinch of salt

Cream together sugar and butter, until light and fluffy. Add coconut extract, pineapple topping, and eggs. Combine until well mixed.

In a separate bowl, combine flour, baking powder, baking soda, coconut, and salt. Toss to combine. Gently add to wet ingredients. Using a small cookie scoop, place dough 2 inches apart on a greased cookie sheet. Bake at 350 degrees for 8–10 minutes. These cookies will remain light in color. Remove from oven and cool completely. Frost cookies with Coconut Glaze.

1½ cups powdered sugar

2 Tbsp. melted butter

¼ cup pineapple juice, or more to taste

3 Tbsp. milk

1 tsp. coconut extract

½ cup flaked coconut

Coconut Glaze

Whisk together powdered sugar, butter, juice, milk, and coconut extract until no lumps appear. Drizzle over cooled Piña Colada cookies and sprinkle with flaked coconut.

Make Some Whoopie Pies

Make Some Whoopie Pies

This cookie is classic, fun, and super easy to make. By switching food coloring to various colors, you can custom make these cookies every time.

½ cup butter, soft

1 cup brown sugar

1 egg

1 tsp. vanilla

2 Tbsp. food coloring

½ cup milk

3 Tbsp. cocoa

2¾ cup flour

½ tsp. baking soda

Vanilla Butter Cream Frosting (see page 19)

1 (7-oz.) jar marshmallow creme

Cream together butter and sugar until light and fluffy. Add egg, vanilla, food coloring, and milk.

In a separate bowl, combine dry ingredients. Gently add dry ingredients into wet and mix until just combined. Drop onto parchment lined cookie sheet in 1-inch balls, using cookie scoop. Batter will be really thick.

Bake at 375 degrees for 8–10 minutes. Remove from oven and cool completely. Frost middle of half of the batch of cookies with Vanilla Buttercream Frosting, folding in marshmallow creme first. Top with remaining half of cookies. Store leftover cookies in an airtight container for up to 5 days—*if* they last that long.

Cherry Chocolate Cookies

This cookie is perfect for chocolate and cherry lovers.

12 oz. semi-sweet chocolate

½ cup butter

½ cup sugar

¼ cup dark brown sugar

2 eggs

2 Tbsp. cocoa

½ tsp. salt

1 tsp. baking powder

1 cup flour

1½ cups dried cherries

Cut chocolate into small pieces. Melt butter and chocolate in the microwave 20 seconds at a time, stirring in between. Once melted and smooth, add sugars and stir to combine. Add eggs and stir again.

Whisk together cocoa, salt, baking powder, and flour. Add semi-sweet chocolate and cherries. Refrigerate dough 45 minutes. Scoop cold dough evenly onto baking sheet and bake at 350 degrees for 11–13 minutes. Do not overbake.

Grandma Lu's Persimmon Cookies

Growing up in California, we had a tradition with my grandma. We would pick these beautiful fruits and then make cookies. Persimmon cookies are unique and delicious. Never underestimate the power of a good tradition —or cookie.

1 tsp. baking soda

1 cup mashed persimmon pulp

½ cup shortening

1 cup sugar

1 egg, beaten

2 cups flour

1 cup chopped nuts

1 cup raisins

½ tsp. cinnamon

½ tsp. cloves

½ tsp. nutmeg

In a small bowl, mix together baking soda and persimmon pulp. Set aside.

Cream together shortening, sugar, and beaten egg. Add persimmon mixture to creamed sugar mix until combined.

In a separate bowl, mix together flour, nuts, raisins, and spices. Add dry ingredients to wet ingredients. Blend well, but do not overmix. Drop by tablespoonful onto parchment lined or greased cookie sheet.

Bake at 350 degrees for 12–14 minutes. Remove from oven and cool cookies completely on a wire rack.

Almond Wedding Cookies

Almond Wedding Cookies

Traditional wedding cookie with a not-so-traditional flavor.
These cookies are updated for the next generation bride.

1½ cups butter, softened

1½ cups powdered sugar

2 tsp. almond extract

2 tsp. vanilla

pinch of salt

1½ cups almonds, ground

2¾ cups flour

Cream butter and sugar together. Add extracts, salt, and almonds. Carefully add flour and stir until combined.

Roll dough into 1-inch balls and bake at 325 degrees for 15 minutes. Do not brown cookies. Roll warm cookies in powdered sugar to coat.

Mini Peanut Butter Bites

Mini Peanut Butter Bites

My neighbor brought me some cookies with a peanut butter cup inside. They were still slightly warm. Needless to say, I hid these cookies and ate every single one myself. Just thinking of them makes my mouth water. I'd better add mini peanut butter cups to my grocery list this week!

½ cup butter

½ cup brown sugar, lightly packed

½ cup sugar

½ cup creamy peanut butter

1 egg

2 tsp. vanilla

1½ Tbsp. water

½ tsp. baking soda

½ tsp. baking powder

1¾ cups flour

40 mini peanut butter cups, unwrapped

Cream butter, sugars, and peanut butter until smooth and fluffy. Add egg, vanilla, and water.

In a separate bowl, combine baking soda, baking powder, and flour. Gently combine dry ingredients with wet until mixed.

Place 1 tablespoon of rounded cookie dough in a well greased mini muffin tin. Bake at 375 for 7–9 minutes. Remove from oven and carefully place a mini peanut butter cup in the middle, pressing down. Allow cookie to cool completely before removing from the muffin tin. Hide some of these cookies for later.

Amish Cookies

Amish Cookies

Amish cookies never cease to please a crowd. They bake up perfectly every time.

1 cup sugar

1 cup butter

1 cup vegetable oil

2 eggs

1 tsp. vanilla

4½ cups flour

1 tsp. baking soda

1 cup powdered sugar

1 tsp. cream of tartar

Combine sugar, butter, and oil. Mix until combined well. Add eggs and vanilla and mix again until combined. Add dry ingredients.

Drop 1½-inch pieces on a greased cookie sheet. Flatten cookie slightly with the bottom of a glass. Bake at 375 degrees for 10 minutes. Remove from oven and cool. Do not overbake these cookies, or they will become hard.

Oatmeal Butterscotch

Oatmeal Butterscotch Cookies

My dad loves butterscotch chips in a variety of things like cupcakes and cookies.
This cookie is especially for him.

1 cup butter

¾ cup brown sugar

½ cup white sugar

2 eggs

2 tsp. vanilla

1½ cups flour

½ tsp. baking soda

pinch of salt

3 cups quick oats

2 cups butterscotch chips

1 cup chopped pecans or
  walnuts (optional)

Cream butter and sugars together until light and fluffy. Add eggs and vanilla.

In a separate bowl, combine flour, baking soda, salt, and oats. Quickly stir to combine. Gently add flour mixture to the wet mixture mix until just combined. Fold in butterscotch chips and nuts (optional).

Drop batter by tablespoonful onto greased cookie sheets. Bake at 375 degrees for 8–10 minutes. Remove before completely done. Allow cookies to rest on baking sheet for 1–2 minutes. Transfer cookies to a wire rack to cool completely.

Julia's Molasses Cookies

I remember as a child sitting in my grandmother's kitchen, rolling this cookie dough into balls and dipping them in sugar. What a happy memory it is for me, to have been taught how to bake by an incredible woman. We also ate quite a bit of raw cookie dough. I'm sure my grandma knew that we would, but we still always had plenty to bake.

¾ cup shortening

1 cup sugar

¼ cup molasses

1 egg

2 tsp. baking soda

2 cups flour

½ tsp. cloves

1 tsp. cinnamon

½ tsp. ginger

½ tsp. salt

decorating sugar

Melt shortening in a small pot over medium heat until liquid. Remove from heat and cool.

Add sugar, molasses, and egg. Mix until combined and smooth. Sift dry ingredients together and add to wet. Carefully combine together, not overmixing.

Refrigerate for 1 hour, covered. Roll chilled dough into 1-inch balls, and roll in decorating sugar. Place on a lightly greased cookie sheet and bake at 375 degrees for 6 minutes. Remove from oven and let stand on hot cookie sheet for 1–2 minutes. Then place the cookies on a wire rack to cool completely. Store these cooled cookies in an airtight container to keep soft.

Sunny Lemonade Cookies

I am a huge fan of lemons. Lemons are sweet and tangy, and sometimes sweet.

1 cup sugar

1 cup butter

2 eggs

½ cup lemonade concentrate, plus ¼ cup for glaze

1 tsp. lemon juice

2 drops yellow food coloring

2 Tbsp. grated lemon zest

3 cups flour

1 tsp. baking soda

pinch of salt

decorating sugars (optional)

Cream together sugar and butter until light and fluffy. Add eggs, ½ cup lemonade concentrate, lemon juice, food coloring, and lemon zest. Mix until well combined and fragrant.

In a separate bowl, combine flour, baking soda, and salt. Add dry ingredients to wet, and stir until combined.

Drop onto a greased cookie sheet and bake at 400 degrees for 8–10 minutes. Remove from oven and brush with remaining lemonade concentrate. Sprinkle with decorating sugar if desired.

Cowboy Up

Cowboy Up

This cookie has everything in it except the kitchen sink. Delicious!

1½ cups whole wheat flour

½ cup flour

1 tsp. baking soda

1 tsp. baking powder

1 tsp. cinnamon

½ tsp. salt

½ cup sugar

½ cup brown sugar

¾ cup butter, softened

3 egg whites

½ tsp. vanilla

1 cup chocolate chips

½ cup quick oats

1 cup shredded coconut

½ cup Craisins

1 cup chopped nuts
(optional)

Mix together flours, baking soda, baking powder, cinnamon, and salt. Set aside.

In a large bowl, beat sugars and butter until light and creamy. Add eggs and vanilla and beat until combined. Add chocolate chips, oats, coconut, Craisins, and nuts. Add flour mixture a little at a time.

Drop by 2-tablespoon scoop onto a greased baking sheet. Bake at 350 degrees for 10–12 minutes. Remove from oven and cool completely.

Double Chocolate Chip S'more

Double Chocolate Chip

Double Chocolate Chip Candy Cane

Double Chocolate Chip Cookies

Chocolate cookie dough with white chocolate chips. Double chocolate in every bite!

¼ cup sugar

¾ cup brown sugar

1 cup butter, softened

2 eggs

1 tsp. vanilla

1 (4-oz.) pkg. chocolate instant pudding mix (powder only)

1 tsp. baking soda

2¼ cups flour

2 cups white chocolate chips

Cream together sugars and butter until light and fluffy. Add eggs, vanilla, and pudding mix.

In a separate bowl, mix together baking soda and flour. Gently add to wet ingredients. Fold in chocolate chips.

Use a small cookie scoop to drop dough onto lightly greased cookie sheet. Bake at 350 degrees for 8–10 minutes, until sides become golden. Remove from oven and cool completely on a wire rack.

RECIPE CONTINUES ON THE FOLLOWING PAGE

Variations

S'more: Prepare as directed above. Omit white chocolate chips. Add 1 cup mini marshmallows, 1 cup dark chocolate chips, and 1 cup crushed graham crackers. Bake according to directions. Remove from oven and cool completely.

Mint Patty: Prepare as directed above. Omit white chocolate chips. Add ½ teaspoon mint extract. Top cookie with mint patty when removing from oven and gently press down to secure patty. Allow cookies to cool. Drizzle with melted white chocolate.

Candy Cane: Prepare and bake as directed above. Remove cookies from oven. Gently press down cookie with the bottom of a glass to flatten. Allow cookies to cool completely. Using 1 cup crushed peppermint candy and 1 cup melted white chocolate, frost cookies with warm melted chocolate and sprinkle with crushed candy canes.

Chocolate Sandwich Cookie: Prepare and bake as directed above. Omit white chocolate chips. Remove cookies from oven. Gently press down cookie with the bottom of a glass to flatten. Allow cookies to cool completely. Frost the bottom side of one cookie with Vanilla Buttercream Frosting (see page 19), and place frosted side together with another cookie to make a sandwich.

German Chocolate: Prepare and bake cookie as directed above. Omit white chocolate chips. Remove from oven and cool completely. Meanwhile, heat 1 cup shredded coconut, 2 tablespoons butter, ¼ cup cream, and ½ cup brown sugar in a skillet, stirring until slightly thickened. Cool and frost cookie with coconut frosting and top with grated chocolate or mini chocolate chips.

Creamy Lemon Blueberry Delight

Lemons. Blueberries. Delicious. Satisfying. Tasty.

6 Tbsp. unsalted
  butter, melted

2 cups graham cracker
  crumbs (about 12
  graham crackers)

2 (8-oz.) packages cream
  cheese, softened

2 large eggs

½ cup sugar

1 tsp. lemon juice

1 Tbsp. grated
  lemon zest

1 tsp. pure vanilla

1 (10-oz.) jar blueberry jam,
  warmed

1 cup fresh blueberries

Preheat oven to 350 degrees. Mix together butter and graham cracker crumbs until blended. Press down into a 9 × 13 baking dish. Place in refrigerator.

In a large bowl, beat cream cheese until smooth. Add eggs, sugar, lemon juice, lemon zest, and vanilla. Beat well to combine. Spread warmed jam over crust in an even layer. Top with fresh blueberries. Pour cream cheese layer over the top and spread evenly.

Bake for 30 minutes until slightly set and puffy. Remove and cool to room temperature. Cover and refrigerate until cold. Cut into squares.

Luscious Lemon Bars

Luscious Lemon Bars

Lemon has such a perfect flavor—light and sweet, fresh and clean.
My great editor and friend Stacy loves lemons. This recipe is just for her.
Thanks for all the wonderful insight. You are amazing!

½ cup butter, softened

2 Tbsp. grated lemon zest

1 cup plus 3 Tbsp. flour, divided

¼ cup powdered sugar

3 eggs

3 Tbsp. lemon juice

¾ tsp. baking powder

1½ cups sugar

Combine butter, 1 tablespoon lemon zest, 1 cup flour, and powdered sugar in a food processor. Process until mixture becomes a crumb texture.

Press crumbs into a greased 8×8 baking dish. Spread evenly to form a crust. Bake at 350 degrees for 15 minutes.

Meanwhile, beat eggs, lemon juice, remaining flour, baking powder, and lemon zest and sugar. Pour over baked crust and bake for 25 more minutes. Remove from oven and cool. Dust with powdered sugar and cut into squares.

Key Lime Surprise

I am a firm believer of variety in both life and desserts.
Here is a great key lime bar that really shines.

½ cup butter, softened

1 cup flour

½ cup powdered sugar

2 Tbsp. lime zest

3 egg yolks

2–3 drops green food
coloring

1 can sweetened
condensed milk

½ cup key lime juice

lime zest for garnish

Combine butter, flour, powdered sugar, and 1 tablespoon lime zest in a food processor. Process until mixture becomes a crumb texture. Press crumbs into a greased 8×8 baking dish. Spread evenly to form a crust. Bake at 350 degrees for 15 minutes.

Beat egg yolks, food coloring, and sweetened condensed milk until well combined. Add key lime juice and 1 tablespoon lime zest. Put over crust and bake for 15 more minutes until custard is set. Remove from oven and cool. Sprinkle with lime zest for garnish and cut into squares. Refrigerate leftover bars.

Heavenly Almond Bars

My sister-in-law has a tradition of making almond cake at Christmastime. I thought I'd make it into a cookie bar. Not only will you have your cake and eat it too, but you can also have your cookie bar and eat it too.

1 cup butter

1¼ cups sugar

1 egg

1½ tsp. pure almond extract

⅔ cup milk

¾ cup flour

½ cup almond flour (process ½ cup slivered almonds in your food processor)

½ cup slivered almonds

Cream together butter and sugar until light and fluffy. Add egg, almond extract, and milk. Combine until smooth. Fold in flour and almond flour. Mix until combined. Spread batter evenly on a greased 9×9 baking dish, lined with parchment paper and grease again (optional). Top with slivered almonds.

Bake at 350 degrees for 30 minutes. Remove and sprinkle with remaining slivered almonds. Bake for 20–25 minutes longer, until almonds are golden and cake tests done with a toothpick. Cool completely and cut into squares.

Magically Delicious

Magically Delicious

My cousin's husband made these for a family party. Their plate of magic bars disappeared before anything else. They are terrific! These are easy to make, and you can keep the items for these bars in your pantry for a last minute treat.

½ cup butter

1½ cup graham cracker crumbs

1 can sweetened condensed milk (you can use fat-free)

1½ cups flaked coconut

¾ cup peanut butter chips

1 cup chopped nuts (almonds, walnuts, or peanuts)

Preheat oven to 350 degrees. Melt butter in a 9×9 baking dish. Top with graham crackers. Layer with sweetened condensed milk, coconut, peanut butter chips, and nuts. Press down firmly.

Bake for 25 minutes, until golden. Remove from oven and cool completely. Cut into squares.

Crazy for Cranberries

Crazy for Cranberries

With the sweetness of these bars and the rich flavor, you won't be able to eat just one! I also call these cookie bars the "visit your dentist more often" cookie bars. Enjoy every single bite!

1 cup butter

1 cup brown sugar

3 eggs

1 tsp. vanilla

¼ tsp. salt

1 tsp. nutmeg

1½ cups flour

1 cup dried cranberries, minced and divided

½ cup white chocolate, chopped fine

Preheat oven to 350 degrees. In a large bowl, cream together butter and sugar until light and fluffy. Add eggs, vanilla, salt, and nutmeg. Stir in flour. Add ½ cup dried cranberries and chopped chocolate. Fold into batter. Line 9×13 baking dish with parchment paper and overlap the edges to make for easy removal. Grease generously. Place batter evenly and spread to all corners. Bake in oven for 20–25 minutes or until lightly golden. Remove from oven and cool completely before frosting with Cream Cheese Frosting. Sprinkle with remaining cranberries and top with White Chocolate Drizzle.

Cream Cheese Frosting

8 oz. cream cheese, softened

½ cup butter, softened

1 tsp. vanilla

3¾ cups powdered sugar

Beat cream cheese until light and fluffy. Add butter and vanilla. Add powdered sugar, and mix until light and fluffy. Spread generously over cranberry bars. Sprinkle with remaining cranberries.

White Chocolate Drizzle

½ cup white chocolate chips

1 Tbsp. vegetable oil

Combine ingredients and microwave 20 seconds at a time, stirring in between until smooth. Drizzle over frosting and cranberries. Cut into squares.

Melt in Your Mouth Maple Bars

I love getting ideas from friends and family. This recipe was an inspiration from my good friend Carol. She is a delight and knows a good maple bar when she tastes one. Thanks!

½ cup maple syrup (natural is best)

½ cup butter

½ cup sugar

1 egg

⅔ cup flour

1 cup quick oats

1 cup chopped nuts (almond or walnuts)

¾ tsp. baking powder

1 tsp. vanilla

Mix together all ingredients. Place in a greased 8×8 baking dish. Bake at 350 degrees for 30–35 minutes or until golden brown. Cut into squares while warm.

Southern Sweet Potato Bars

Sometimes I feel as though I am a southern girl at heart. The sweet and savory flavors make my mouth water and my stomach want more. Here is a simple yet flavorful bar recipe.

½ cup brown sugar

6 Tbsp. butter,
   softened

1 egg

1 tsp. vanilla

1 tsp. orange zest

½ cup mashed sweet potato

1¼ cups flour

1 tsp. cinnamon

1¼ tsp. baking powder

½ cup pecans, toasted
   and chopped, divided
   (optional)

Cream together sugar and butter until light and fluffy. Add egg, vanilla, orange zest, and sweet potato. Combine all dry ingredients and gradually beat into wet ingredients. Pour batter into 9×9 greased and parchment-lined baking dish.

Bake at 350 degrees for 23–25 minutes, or until a toothpick comes out clean. Remove from oven and cool. Top with maple glaze.

1 Tbsp. milk

½ tsp. maple extract

2 cups powdered sugar

Maple Glaze
Whisk all ingredients together until all lumps are gone. Drizzle on top of cooled bars. Sprinkle with toasted pecans for added garnish and texture.

Caramel Apple Bars

Caramel Apple Bars

Caramel apples sound good, especially in the fall. Try this cookie bar.
You're sure to make it again and again and again.

1 cup butter, softened

1 cup brown sugar

2 cups flour

2 cups quick cooking oats

1 tsp. baking soda

2 cups Granny Smith
   apples, diced

1 cup walnuts or pecans,
   chopped

1 small jar caramel topping

Preheat oven to 350 degrees. Melt butter and sugar, and add flour, oats, and baking soda. Mix together until dough crumbles. Press half of dough mixture into a small jelly roll pan.

Bake for 7–10 minutes. Remove from oven. Arrange apples and nuts on top of crust. Pour caramel sauce over top and sprinkle remaining dough mixture over entire caramel sauce. Bake 10–12 minutes longer until dough is slightly golden. Remove and cool completely. Cut into squares.

Best of All Pumpkin Bars

This recipe is a mixture of my three favorite pumpkin bars that I make. This one has the best flavor, is easiest to make, and takes the least amount of time. Sprinkle with powdered sugar when cooled.

2 cups flour

1 tsp. cinnamon

½ tsp. nutmeg

2 tsp. baking powder

1 tsp. salt

1 tsp. soda

1 (4-oz) pkg. coconut cream
    instant pudding
    (powder only)

1 (16-oz.) can pumpkin puree

3 eggs, beaten

½ cup oil

1 cup sugar

In a large bowl, mix together all dry ingredients. Add pumpkin, eggs, oil, and sugar. Gently fold ingredients together until combined.

Spread batter in a greased small jelly roll pan and bake at 350 degrees for 20–25 minutes or until set in the middle. Remove from oven and cool completely. Dust with powdered sugar.

Perfectly Peanut Butter Bars

Need I say more? I still think that chocolate and peanut butter go hand in hand. These bars are soft and chewy with chocolate melted on top. Remember not to overcook these little treats! I don't think my family has ever been able to wait until they have completely cooled to try them.

1 cup butter, softened

½ cup sugar

½ cup brown sugar

1 Tbsp. vanilla

⅔ cup peanut butter

2 eggs, beaten

1¾ cups whole wheat flour

2 cups quick cooking oats

1 tsp. baking soda

1 (12-oz.) package chocolate chips

Cream together butter, sugars, vanilla, and peanut butter. Add eggs one at a time until well blended.

In a separate bowl, mix together all dry ingredients and add slowly to wet ingredients. Stir until just blended. Place batter in a large greased jelly roll pan, spreading evenly.

Bake at 350 degrees for 15 minutes. Remove from oven and sprinkle chocolate chips over hot cookie. Allow chocolate to stand for 2 minutes, spreading once they have softened. Cool completely before cutting into 1½-inch squares.

Christmas Cherry Bars

Christmas Cherry Bars

While I was growing up, my mother always made cherry almond cookies for Christmas. We would eat the cookie dough and cherries before they ever made it to the oven. She had to double the batch to make enough for the neighbors. This cookie bar is still a tradition in our family.

1 cup butter, softened

1 cup sugar

2 eggs

1½ tsp. almond extract, divided

2½ cups flour

1 tsp. salt

1 jar Maraschino cherries, cut in half and stems removed

1 Tbsp. milk

2 cups powdered sugar

Cream together butter, sugar, and eggs. Add 1 teaspoon almond extract. Slowly beat in flour and salt. Spread batter over a greased cookie sheet or smaller jelly roll pan. Sprinkle batter with cherries.

Bake at 350 degrees for 15–18 minutes until lightly golden but soft. Remove from oven and cool. Mix together milk, ½ teaspoon almond extract, and powdered sugar. Whisk together until there are no more lumps.

Drizzle over cooled cookie bars. Cut into 1½-inch squares and serve. This recipe freezes well without the glaze.

Traditional Nanaimo Bars

Traditional Nanaimo Bars

While in British Columbia with my husband on business, we came across these sinful treats at a small deli by our hotel. After we came home, I decided to make this recipe all my own. Here's my best version of this great Canadian favorite.

Crust

2 Tbsp. cocoa

½ cup unsalted butter

½ cup sugar

1 egg, beaten

1½ cups graham cracker crumbs

½ cup coconut

½ cup almonds, chopped

Melt cocoa, butter, and sugar. Whisk in egg. Continue to stir until sauce thickens. Remove from heat and allow to cool for 5 minutes. Add graham cracker crumbs, coconut, and almonds. Pat down evenly in the bottom of a 9×13 greased baking dish. Place in freezer to set and harden while making the middle.

Middle

1 cup butter, softened

⅓ cup heavy cream

¼ cup Bird's custard powder

3 cups powdered sugar

Cream together butter and heavy cream. Add custard powder and sugar and blend until smooth and creamy. Spread over hardened crust. Return to freezer to set.

Topping:

8 oz. semi-sweet chocolate

4 Tbsp. butter

Melt and mix together chocolate and butter. Cool slightly. Pour and spread gently over custard filling. Allow bars to harden completely before cutting.

Coconut Pecan Pie Bars

This classic pie recipe is even better as a cookie bar. With a sweet shortbread crust, thick sugar middle, and toasted pecans on top, it's hard to wait until these bars are cooled before grabbing a fork.

2 cups flour

¾ cup butter, cold

1 cup powdered sugar

5 eggs

1 cup corn syrup

pinch of salt

2 tsp. vanilla

1 cup white sugar

½ cup brown sugar

3 Tbsp. butter, melted

3½ cups chopped pecans

¾–1 cup coconut

In a large bowl, combine flour, butter, and powdered sugar. Using a pastry cutter or two knives, cut butter into sugar and flour until butter is pea sized. Spread evenly on the bottom of a 9×13 pan, and bake at 350 degrees for 15–17 minutes.

Meanwhile, whisk together eggs, corn syrup, salt, vanilla, sugars, and melted butter. Pour onto hot crust and top with chopped pecans. Sprinkle with coconut. Return to oven and bake for 25–28 more minutes. Remove from oven and cool completely. Cut into squares.

Triple Chocolate Fudge Brownies

This brownie is so rich, you might only be able to eat just one! It has chocolate, chocolate, and chocolate. Did I mention it has a lot of chocolate inside? If you are in the mood for a great chocolate treat, this is your kind of brownie.

½ cup butter

1 (12-oz.) bag dark chocolate (or semi-sweet) chips

1 cup brown sugar

3 eggs

pinch of salt

½ cup flour

1 cup white chocolate chips

1½ cup milk chocolate chips

In a large saucepan, melt butter and dark chocolate chips on low, stirring frequently. Remove from heat and stir in sugar until well combined. Add eggs, one at a time, stirring in between. Add salt and flour and mix until no flour is seen. Fold in white chocolate chips.

Pour batter into a greased 9×13 baking dish. Bake at 350 degrees for 24–28 minutes until middle is set. Remove from oven and place milk chocolate chips on top of brownies. Let stand for 2 minutes. Spread melted chocolate until smooth. Cool completely and cut into small squares.

Black Forest Brownies
with Cherry Pie Filling Drizzle

Black Forest Brownies

Chocolate and cherries are a timeless classic, and this recipe couldn't be easier. By just adding a scoop of your favorite vanilla ice cream, you can make it speak "perfection."

½ cup butter

1 (12-oz.) bag dark chocolate (or semi-sweet) chips

1 cup brown sugar

3 eggs

pinch of salt

1¼ cup flour

1 (16-oz.) can cherry pie filling

Maraschino cherries (optional)

In a large saucepan, melt butter and dark chocolate chips on low, stirring frequently. Remove from heat and stir in sugar until well combined. Add eggs, one at a time, stirring in between. Add salt and flour and mix until no flour is seen. Gently fold in cherry pie filling.

Pour into a greased and cocoa dusted 9×13 baking dish. Bake at 350 degrees for 25–28 minutes until middle is set but not overdone. Remove from oven and cool completely. Cut into pieces, and top with a Maraschino cherry (optional) or cherry pie filling.

Better to Be Blonde

Blondes do have more fun. Just ask my friend Stacy! These blonde
brownies are delicious and are soft, chewy, and do not dry out.
I am making myself hungry thinking about how good these brownies are!

¾ cup butter

2 cups dark brown sugar, packed

2 eggs, beaten

1 tsp. vanilla

1 tsp. baking powder

1 tsp. baking soda

pinch of salt

2½ cups flour

To melted butter, add sugar and eggs, mixing to combine. Add vanilla and all dry ingredients. Pour batter into a greased 9×9 baking pan. Bake for 20–25 minutes until middle is set but soft. Remove from oven and cool completely before cutting into squares.

Variations

Coconut **Blondies:** Omit vanilla. Add 1 teaspoon coconut extract and 1 cup shredded coconut to recipe. Bake as directed.

Butterscotch **Blondies:** Add 1 cup butterscotch chips to batter. Bake as directed.

White **Chocolate Macadamia Blondies:** Add 1 cup white chocolate chips and 1 cup chopped macadamia nuts to batter. Bake as directed.

Chocolate Caramel Brownies

Warm caramel and warm chocolate brownies are like two peas in a pod. These brownies are delicious.

½ cup butter

1 (12-oz.) bag dark chocolate (or semi-sweet) chips

1 cup brown sugar

3 eggs

pinch of salt

½ cup flour

1 pkg. Kraft caramels, unwrapped

In a large saucepan, melt butter and dark chocolate chips on low, stirring frequently. Remove from heat and stir in sugar until well combined. Add eggs, one at a time, stirring in between. Add salt and flour and mix until no flour is seen.

Pour the batter into a greased and cocoa dusted 9×9 baking pan. Meanwhile, warm caramels according to package directions. Pour warm caramel over brownie batter. Swirl caramel and batter together using a butter knife. Bake at 350 degrees for 25–28 minutes until middle is set. Remove from oven. Cool completely before cutting into squares.

Peanut Butter Cup Brownies

You can't have a good brownie recipe and not add peanut butter cups to it. This brownie is sinful, out of this world, crazy good. I dare you to make it for your next baking adventure. Yes, I double dog dare you.

½ cup butter

1 (12-oz.) bag dark chocolate (or semi-sweet) chips

1 cup brown sugar

3 eggs

½ cup flour

pinch of salt

1 bag chocolate peanut butter cups (at least 20) or extra for snacking

1 bag semi-sweet chocolate chips

In a large saucepan, melt butter and dark chocolate chips on low, stirring frequently. Remove from heat and stir in sugar until well combined. Add eggs, one at a time, stirring in between. Add flour and salt, and mix until no flour is seen.

Pour ⅓ batter into a 9×9 greased and cocoa dusted baking dish. Layer batter with unwrapped chocolate peanut butter cups. Top with remaining brownie batter. Bake at 350 for 25–28 minutes. Remove from oven and top with semi-sweet chips. Allow chips to melt for 2 minutes. Spread chocolate chips evenly for frosting. Cool completely and cut into squares.

Give Me S'more Brownies

Marshmallows, graham cracker crumbs, and chocolate on top of a chewy, rich brownie.

½ cup butter

1 (12-oz.) bag dark chocolate (or semi-sweet) chips

1 cup brown sugar

3 eggs

½ cup flour

pinch of salt

1 cup mini marshmallows

½ cup crushed graham crackers

1 cup chocolate chunks

In a large saucepan, melt butter and dark chocolate chips on low, stirring frequently. Remove from heat and stir in sugar until well combined. Add eggs, one at a time, stirring in between. Add flour and salt, and mix until no flour is seen.

Pour into a greased and cocoa dusted (optional) 9×13 baking dish. Bake at 350 degrees for 20 minutes, placing marshmallows, graham cracker crumbs, and chocolate on top. Return to oven for 5 more minutes until middle is set but not overdone. Remove from oven and cool completely. Once cooled, cut into squares.

Sinful Chocolate Raspberry Brownies

This recipe has me speechless. I really don't know what to do,
except sit down, hold on, and take a bite.

½ cup butter

1 (12-oz.) bag dark chocolate
(or semi-sweet) chips

½ cup seedless raspberry
preserves

1 cup brown sugar

1 tsp. raspberry extract

3 eggs

pinch of salt

¾ cup flour

½ tsp. baking powder

fresh raspberries for garnish

In a large saucepan, melt butter and dark chocolate chips on low, stirring frequently. Whisk in raspberry preserves. Remove from heat and stir in sugar and extract until well combined. Add eggs, one at a time, stirring in between. Add salt, flour, and baking powder. Mix until no flour is seen.

Pour batter into a greased 9×13 baking dish. Bake at 350 degrees for 24–28 minutes until middle is set. Remove from oven to cool, and make the raspberry glaze.

½ cup heavy cream

½ cup seedless raspberry
preserves

1 cup semi-sweet
chocolate chips

Raspberry Glaze

In a small saucepan, simmer cream and preserves until smooth and melted. Remove from heat and add chocolate chips. Pour over cooled brownies. Top with fresh raspberries and refrigerate for 10–15 minutes until the glaze is set. Cut into squares.

Little Turtles

Little Turtles

Hidden layers of caramel, nuts, and chocolate make a good surprise for anyone.
Eat these brownies warm or cold.

½ cup butter

1 (12-oz.) bag dark chocolate (or semi-sweet) chips

1 cup brown sugar

3 eggs

½ cup flour

pinch of salt

1 jar caramel ice cream topping

1 cup pecans, whole or chopped

1 cup chocolate chips

In a large saucepan, melt butter and dark chocolate chips on low, stirring frequently. Remove from heat and stir in sugar until well combined. Add eggs, one at a time, stirring in between. Add flour and salt and mix until no flour is seen. Pour ⅓ batter into a 9×9 greased and cocoa dusted baking dish. Layer batter with 1 cup caramel sauce and pecans. Sprinkle chocolate chips evenly over batter.

Top with remaining batter and bake at 350 degrees for 30–35 minutes. Remove from oven and cool completely before cutting into squares. This brownie will be soft and chewy. Top each cut brownie with a whole pecan and drizzle with remaining caramel sauce.

Mint Patty Brownies

This traditional brownie has a thick and rich texture, with a strong mint flavor.
It is one of my favorite brownies.

½ cup butter

1 (12-oz.) bag dark chocolate
(or semi-sweet) chips

1 cup brown sugar

3 eggs

pinch of salt

1 cup flour

1 bag (16 oz) mint patties,
unwrapped

1½ cups mint
chocolate chips

In a large saucepan, melt butter and dark chocolate chips on low, stirring frequently. Remove from heat and stir in sugar until well combined. Add eggs, one at a time, stirring in between. Add salt and flour, and mix until no flour is seen. Pour half the batter into a greased 9×9 baking sheet lined with parchment paper, leaving paper overlapping the sides. Layer mint patties on an angle, slightly overlapping one another in rows, until all the batter is covered. Top with remaining brownie batter.

Bake at 325 degrees for 25–28 minutes until middle is set but not overdone. Remove from oven and top with mint chocolate chips. After 2 minutes, spread chocolate chips for frosting. Cool completely and lift out of pan, using parchment paper as handles, and cut into squares.

Mayan Fudge Brownies

Spicy, cinnamon, and dark chocolate all in a brownie.
This makes every taste bud in my mouth smile.

½ cup butter

1 (12-oz.) bag dark chocolate (or semi-sweet) chips

1 cup brown sugar

3 eggs

pinch of salt

½ tsp. cayenne pepper

1 tsp. cinnamon

½ cup flour

1 bag milk chocolate chips

In a large saucepan, melt butter and dark chocolate chips on low, stirring frequently. Remove from heat and stir in sugar until well combined. Add eggs, one at a time, stirring in between. Add salt, spices, and flour, and mix until no flour is seen.

Pour batter into a greased and cocoa (optional) dusted 9×9 baking pan. Bake at 350 degrees for 25–28 minutes or until middle is set. Remove from oven. Sprinkle milk chocolate chips on top of hot brownies. Allow chips to melt for 2 minutes. Spread chocolate chips evenly for frosting. Cool completely and cut into squares.

Nutty Bunch Brownies

Nutty Bunch Brownies

Nuts are healthy. So when I make a treat with nuts inside,
I like to consider my treat healthier. Here's to a "healthier" brownie!

½ cup butter

1 (12-oz.) bag dark chocolate (or semi-sweet) chips

1 cup brown sugar

3 eggs

½ cup flour

pinch of salt

1 cup almonds, walnuts, or pecans, chopped (or a mixture of all)

cocoa

powdered sugar

In a large saucepan, melt butter and chocolate chips on low, stirring frequently. Remove from heat and stir in sugar until well combined. Add eggs, one at a time, stirring in between. Add flour and salt, and mix until no flour is seen. Fold in nuts, until combined.

Pour batter into a greased 9×9 baking pan dusted with cocoa. Bake at 350 degrees for 25–28 minutes, until middle is set. Remove from oven. Cool completely, dust with powdered sugar, and cut into squares.

Dreamy Creamy Brownies

This is the classic cream cheese brownie, only this is the best recipe ever. Happy baking!

½ cup butter

1 (12-oz.) bag dark chocolate (or semi-sweet) chips

1 cup brown sugar

3 eggs

½ cup flour

pinch of salt

1 (8-oz.) pkg. cream cheese, softened

1 egg

½ cup sugar

2 Tbsp. flour

In a large saucepan, melt butter and dark chocolate chips on low, stirring frequently. Remove from heat and stir in brown sugar until well combined. Add eggs, one at a time, stirring in between. Add flour and salt, and mix until no flour is seen.

Pour batter into a greased 9×9 baking pan dusted with cocoa. Meanwhile, mix cream cheese, 1 egg, ½ cup sugar, and 2 tablespoons flour, until no lumps appear. Pour cream cheese mixture on top of brownie batter and swirl. Be artistic. Bake at 350 degrees for 25–28 minutes or until middle is set. Remove from oven and cool completely before cutting into squares.

There's Zucchini in Here?

*I always seem to have a plethora of zucchini in my garden, even when I only plant one seed.
I love zucchini, and when I can, I use it in everything I cook or bake, from cakes,
to cookies, to these brownies, I am happy, and my kids love to eat every bite.
I don't feel guilty about sending these brownies in their lunch box to school.*

1 cube butter

1 (12-oz.) bag dark chocolate (or semi-sweet) chips

½ cup brown sugar

½ cup sugar

3 eggs

pinch of salt

1 tsp. cinnamon

1½ cups flour

1 cup grated zucchini, squeezed dry in between paper towels

1 bag milk chocolate chips

1 cup chopped nuts (optional)

In a large saucepan, melt butter and dark chocolate chips on low, stirring frequently. Remove from heat and stir in sugars until well combined. Add eggs, one at a time, stirring in between. Add salt, cinnamon, and flour, and mix until no flour is seen. Fold in grated zucchini.

Pour batter into a greased 9×9 baking pan dusted with cocoa. Bake at 350 degrees for 25–28 minutes, until middle is set. Remove from oven. Sprinkle milk chocolate chips on top of hot brownies. Allow chips to melt for 2 minutes. Spread chocolate chips evenly for frosting. Sprinkle chopped nuts on top of frosting, if desired. Cool completely and cut into squares.

Candy Cane Brownies

Candy Cane Brownies

These brownies are a take on the classic candy cane and chocolate. They are beautiful to look at on a holiday cookie platter and taste so good.

½ cup butter

1 (12-oz.) bag dark chocolate (or semi-sweet) chips

1 cup brown sugar

3 eggs

½ cup flour

pinch of salt

1 bag white chocolate chips

1 cup candy canes, crushed

In a large saucepan, melt butter and chocolate chips on low, stirring frequently. Remove from heat and stir in sugar until well combined. Add eggs, one at a time, stirring in between. Add flour and salt, and mix until no flour is seen.

Pour batter into a greased 9 x 9 baking pan dusted with cocoa. Bake at 350 degrees for 25–28 minutes, until middle is set. Remove from oven.

Sprinkle white chocolate chips on top of hot brownies. Allow chips to melt for 2 minutes. Spread chocolate chips evenly for frosting. Sprinkle with crushed candy canes. Cool completely and cut into squares.

Chocolate Pumpkin Brownies

You can feel a little better knowing there is something good for you in these brownies. The pumpkin flavor is subtle but adds to the richness of this dark chocolate brownie.

½ cups butter

1 (12-oz.) bag dark chocolate (or semi-sweet) chips

1 cup brown sugar

3 eggs

1 cup pumpkin puree

1¼ cup flour

pinch of salt

½ tsp. baking powder

In a large saucepan, melt butter and chocolate chips on low, stirring frequently. Remove from heat and stir in sugar until well combined. Add eggs, one at a time, stirring in between. Add pumpkin puree, flour, salt, and baking powder. Mix until no flour is seen.

Pour batter into a greased 9x9 baking pan dusted with cocoa. Bake at 350 degrees for 25–28 minutes, until middle is set. Remove from oven and cool completely before cutting into squares.

Watching *Your* Waistline

Cookies

Simply Peanut Butter Cookies

Spicy Applesauce Oatmeal Cookies

Whole Wheat Sugar Cookies

Dark Chocolate Chip Cookies

Pumpkin Chocolate Cookies

Butternut Squash Pecan Cookies

Apple Cider Cookies

Olive Oil Shortbread

Brownies

Better Believe It! Brownies

Surprise, Surprise! Brownies

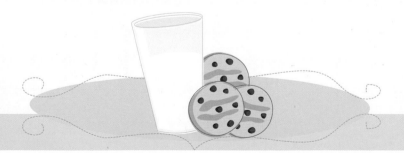

Simply Peanut Butter

Simply Peanut Butter Cookies

This recipe is easy to remember. Two of each ingredient makes these splendid, simple peanut butter cookies.

2 cups natural peanut butter, smooth or chunky

2 cups low calorie sweetener (granular)

2 egg whites

Cream peanut butter and sweetener. Add egg whites. Use a small cookie scoop to drop dough onto a lightly greased cookie sheet. Bake at 350 degrees for 8–10 minutes, until middle appears set. Remove cookies from oven and cool completely on a wire rack.

Spicy Applesauce Oatmeal Cookies

Spicy oatmeal low-fat/low-sugar cookies can have all the flavor and taste of the original cookies, but they are much more healthy for you. Eat one of these cookies without the guilt.

½ cup olive oil

1 cup unsweetened applesauce

3 egg whites

1 tsp. cinnamon

1 tsp. nutmeg

1 tsp. ground cloves

2 Tbsp. ground flax seed

½ cup unsweetened shredded coconut

1 cup whole wheat flour

3 cups quick oats

Cream oil, applesauce, and egg whites until well combined. Add spices, flax seed, and coconut. Stir until combined. Add flour and oats, stirring until just combined.

Drop by small cookie scoop onto a lightly greased baking sheet. Bake at 350 degrees for 8–10 minutes or until golden on the edges. These cookies freeze well and taste better if hand mixed.

Whole Wheat Sugar Cookies

Whole wheat sugar cookies are the favorite at our home.
With or without frosting, these cookies are soft and full of hearty flavor.

1 cup low-fat butter, soft

½ cup agave nectar (or 1 cup sugar substitute)

2 egg whites

3 Tbsp. light sour cream

½ tsp. almond extract

½ tsp. vanilla

2¾ cups whole wheat flour

½ tsp. baking soda

¼ tsp. salt

Cream butter and nectar (or sugar substitute) together. Add eggs, sour cream, almond extract, and vanilla. Mix until combined. Add flour, soda, and salt.

Roll together into a ball and refrigerate covered for 1 hour. Roll out the dough on a floured surface and cut into shapes.

Bake at 375 degrees for 6–8 minutes. These cookies do not brown. Do not overbake. Remove from oven and cool completely. Frost if desired.

Dark Chocolate Chip Cookies

Dark Chocolate Chip Cookies

This low-fat/low-sugar recipe for dark chocolate cookies are out-of-this-world great. Hide some from your family and friends. They are sure to be eaten quickly.

¼ cup low-fat butter

½ cup agave nectar (or ¾ cup sugar substitute)

1 egg white

⅓ cup unsweetened applesauce

1 tsp. vanilla

1¼ cup whole wheat flour

1 tsp. baking soda

pinch of salt

¼ cup cocoa

⅓ cup mini chocolate chips

Cream together, by hand, butter, agave nectar (or sugar substitute), egg, applesauce, and vanilla. Stir in flour, baking soda, salt, and cocoa. Batter will appear crumbly, but keep stirring. Fold in mini chocolate chips.

Use a small cookie scoop to place batter on a lightly greased cookie sheet. Bake at 375 degrees for 7–9 minutes. Remove from oven and allow to cool completely on a wire rack.

Pumpkin Chocolate Cookies

These cookies have left me speechless.

1 cup canned pumpkin

1 cup unsweetened
  applesauce

½ cup agave nectar
  (or ½ cup honey)

1 cup whole wheat flour

1 tsp. baking soda

1½ tsp. pumpkin pie spice

3 cups quick oats

Cream together by hand pumpkin, applesauce, and agave nectar (or honey). Stir in flour, soda, spice, and oats. With a small cookie scoop, drop dough onto a lightly greased cookie sheet. Bake at 350 degrees for 12–15 minutes or until cookies are set in the middle. Remove from oven and allow cookies to cool completely on a wire rack.

Butternut Squash Pecan Cookies

I love butternut squash. It is very versatile. It tastes good in savory dishes or sweet dishes, like this delicious cookie.

½ cup low-fat butter

1 cup sugar substitute

1½ cup cooked and mashed butternut squash

2 egg whites

2¼ cups whole wheat flour

pinch of salt

½ tsp. nutmeg

½ tsp. ginger

2 tsp. cinnamon

1 tsp. baking soda

1 tsp. baking powder

1 cup chopped pecans

Cream together butter and sugar substitute, adding butternut squash and egg whites. Hand stir in dry ingredients until well combined. Fold in chopped pecans.

Drop by tablespoon onto a parchment lined cookie sheet. Bake cookies at 375 degrees for 10 minutes, or until lightly golden on the edges. Remove from oven and cool completely on a wire rack.

Apple Cider Cookies

Apple Cider Cookies

Doesn't this cookie sound delicious? Mouth-watering, soft cookies to eat on a cold fall day. Life is good.

1½ cup low-fat butter spread or margarine

1 cup raw sugar

½ cup unsweetened applesauce

1 (single serving) pkg. sugar-free apple cider mix

2 small Granny Smith apples, cored and diced

pinch of salt

2 cups whole wheat flour

1 tsp. of baking soda

2 Tbsp. flax seed

¾ cups chopped almonds (optional)

Cream butter and sugar together until light and fluffy. Add applesauce, cider mix, apples, and salt. Mix until well combined. Add dry ingredients and stir until just combined, being careful not to over-mix dough. Fold in almonds (optional).

Drop onto lightly greased baking sheets. Bake at 375 degrees for 8–10 minutes. Remove from oven and cool completely.

Olive Oil Shortbread

This cookie has good fat and a sophisticated flavor all its own. Simply good.

1 cup olive oil
1½ cups powdered sugar
3 cups flour

In a mixer, blend all ingredients until dough forms a ball and pulls away from the sides of the bowl. Shape dough into a log on parchment paper and crimp ends (twist like a piece of candy) to seal.

Refrigerate for 30–45 minutes until stiff. With a sharp knife, cut ⅓-inch pieces. Bake at 400 degrees for 8–10 minutes. Edges will slightly be golden. Remove from oven and leave cookies to sit on the cookie sheet for 1–2 minutes before placing on a wire rack to cool. Frost if desired.

Better Believe It! Brownies

Chocolate, rich, and full of fudge flavor, no one will ever guess it's good for you.

---

1 cup low-fat butter, melted

1 cup agave nectar
   (or 1 cup sugar substitute)

½ cup cocoa

3 egg whites

1 tsp. vanilla

1½ cup whole wheat flour

2 Tbsp. ground flax seed

1 cup semi-sweet
   chocolate chips

Whisk together butter, agave nectar (or sugar substitute), and cocoa. Add egg whites and vanilla. Gently fold in flour, flax seed, and chocolate chips.

Bake at 350 degrees for 25–28 minutes or until middle is set. Remove from oven and allow brownies to cool completely. Dust with powdered sugar and cut into squares.

Surprise, Surprise! Brownies

*If you don't believe this, all I ask is that you try it once. I'm not crazy,
just obsessed with baking. I was hooked on this brownie at first bite.*

6 Tbsp. cocoa powder

¾ cup flour

pinch of salt

½ cup agave nectar (or ¾
cup sugar substitute)

½ cup ripe avocado

1 tsp. vanilla

½ cup unsweetened
applesauce

1 egg white

In a small bowl, combine cocoa, flour, and salt. In a separate bowl, combine all wet ingredients and mix until smooth and creamy. Gently add dry ingredients, mixing until just combined.

Pour batter into a parchment lined 9×9 baking pan (with sides overlapping for handles). Bake at 350 degrees for 25–30 minutes, or until middle is set. Remove brownies from oven and cool completely. Sprinkle with powdered sugar and cut into squares.

Gluten-free *and* Flavorful

Cookies
Chocolate Chunky Cookies
Almond Cranberry Cookies
Harvest Pumpkin Cookies
Peanut Butter Bliss
Lemon Drop Cookies
Ginger Chocolate Snaps
Coconut Snowballs
Classic Sugar Cookies

Brownies
Oatmeal Fudge Brownies
Beany Blondies

Bars
My Little Monkeys
No-Bake Peanut Butter Fudge
Cranberry Nut Bars

Chocolate Chunky

Chocolate Chunky Cookies

The traditional chocolate chip cookie has met its match.
This cookie will wow friends and family, and they WILL ask you for this recipe.

½ cup almond oil

½ cup agave nectar

1 tsp. vanilla

⅓ cup unsweetened applesauce

dash of salt

1 tsp. baking soda

1½ cups almond flour

1½ cups rice flour

3 tsp. xanthan gum

2 tsp. cream of tartar

1 cup gluten-free chocolate chunks

With a whisk, stir together almond oil and agave nectar. Add vanilla, applesauce, salt, and baking soda. Gently fold in almond flour, rice flour, xanthan gum, cream of tartar, and chocolate chunks.

Drop by small cookie scoop onto parchment paper and bake at 350 degrees for 8–10 minutes, or until edges are slightly golden. Remove from oven and cool completely.

Variation: for chocolate batter, add ½ cup gluten-free cocoa and increase almond oil to ¾ cup.

Almond Cranberry Cookies

Chocolate, rich and full of fudge flavor, no one will ever guess it's good for you.

3 eggs

½ cup butter, melted

4 Tbsp. honey

1 tsp. vanilla

1 tsp. almond extract

1 cup almond flour

1 cup coconut flour

1 tsp. cream of tartar

1½ tsp. xanthan gum

½ cup chopped almonds (optional)

½ cup dried cranberries

Mix together eggs, butter, and honey until combined. Add vanilla, almond extract, flours, cream of tartar, and xanthan gum. Gently mix until flour is mostly gone. Fold in nuts and cranberries.

Drop by teaspoon onto a greased cookie sheet. Bake at 350 degrees for 10–12 minutes. Remove from oven and cool on a wire rack.

Harvest Pumpkin Cookies

This light cookie with the chocolate and butterscotch chips and creamy pumpkin is to die for. It is a taste of autumn in your mouth.

½ cup butter

1 cup brown sugar

1 tsp. vanilla

1 cup pumpkin puree

2 eggs

½ cup almond flour

1 cup rice flour

4 tsp. baking powder

½ cup potato starch

1½ tsp. xanthan gum

½ tsp. cream of tartar

pinch of salt

2 tsp. pumpkin
pie spice

½ cup gluten-free semi-
sweet chocolate chips

½ cup gluten-free
butterscotch chips

Cream butter and sugar together until light and fluffy. Add vanilla, pumpkin, and eggs, mixing until combined. In a separate bowl, mix together flours, baking powder, potato starch, xanthan gum, cream of tartar, salt, and pumpkin pie spice. Fold in chocolate and butterscotch chips.

Bake at 350 degrees for 12–15 minutes, or until lightly golden. Remove from oven and cool completely on a wire rack.

Peanut Butter Bliss

You don't have to sacrifice taste just because you've chosen to eat gluten-free. Here is a great peanut butter cookie that is soft and chewy.

2 Tbsp. ground flax seed

6 Tbsp. water

½ cup brown sugar, packed

2 cups natural crunchy peanut butter

1 ripe banana, mashed

2 tsp. baking soda

In the microwave, heat flax and water, until thick. Allow to cool. Add sugar, peanut butter, and banana. Combine until mixed together. Add baking soda. Dough will be thick. You can also process this in your food processor.

Bake at 350 degrees for 8–10 minutes or until the cookies are golden. Remove from oven and cool completely on a wire rack.

Lemon Drop Cookies

Yes, lemon drops. They make my mouth water. Sweet, tangy, soft, and delightful, these cookies are a crowd pleaser.

¾ cup almond (or rice) flour

½ cup potato starch

½ tsp. baking powder

pinch of salt

1 tsp. xanthan gum

½ cup sugar

½ cup butter, softened

1 egg

2 Tbsp. lemon zest

1 tsp. lemon extract

1 cup lemon drop candies, crushed

Whisk together dry ingredients. In a separate bowl, cream together butter and sugar until light and fluffy. Add egg, lemon zest, and extract, mixing until combined. Gently add dry ingredients, being careful not to overmix. Fold in crushed lemon drop candies. Roll into balls and press somewhat flat with the bottom of a glass, on a parchment lined cookie sheet.

Bake at 350 degrees for 8–10 minutes. Remove from oven and cool completely on a wire rack.

Ginger Chocolate Snaps

Ginger Chocolate Snaps

My good friend, and sometimes my second brain, told me about a great chocolate and ginger cookie.
So I made this recipe with her in mind. I'm sure it will satisfy your sweet tooth too.
This one is for you my dear. *hugs*

1½ cups butter

1 cup raw sugar

½ cup molasses

2 eggs

4 cups gluten-free flour mix

2 tsp. cinnamon

1½ tsp. ginger

2 tsp. baking soda

2 tsp. baking powder

2 tsp. xanthan gum

1 tsp. cream of tartar

1 cup gluten-free semi-sweet
   mini chocolate chips

decorating sugar for
   rolling cookies

Cream butter and sugar in a large mixer until light and fluffy. Add molasses and eggs and combine well.

In a separate bowl, mix flour, spices, baking soda, baking powder, xanthan gum, and cream of tarter. Whisk until combined. Gently add dry ingredients to wet, and combine until barely mixed. Fold in mini chocolate chips.

Refrigerate for 1 hour until well chilled. Remove dough from refrigerator and roll into 1-inch balls. Dip into decorating sugar and place on a parchment lined cookie sheet. Place 2 inches apart. Bake at 350 degrees for 5–6 minutes for chewy cookies and 7–8 for crispy cookies. Remove from oven and cool completely on a wire rack.

Coconut Snowballs

Fast and easy, I usually have all the ingredients in my pantry. These cookies are simple and cost efficient, which I tend to like more and more these days.

4 egg whites

⅓ cup sugar

4 cups shredded coconut

dash of ground nutmeg

pinch of salt

1 tsp. coconut extract

6 Tbsp. cornstarch or potato starch

Beat egg whites until soft peaks form. Gradually add sugar while beating to create stiff peaks.

In a separate bowl, mix together coconut, nutmeg, salt, extract, and cornstarch. Fold one half of the coconut mixture at a time into egg whites gently so that your egg whites don't fall.

Using a small cookie scoop, place dough onto parchment paper and bake at 350 degrees for 10–12 minutes or until cookies turn light golden in color. Remove from oven and cool completely on a wire rack.

Classic Sugar Cookies

Delicious. Easy. Fast.

2½ cups rice flour

1 tsp. baking powder

2½ tsp. xanthan gum

1 tsp. cream of tartar

1 cup sugar

1 cup butter

1 egg

2 tsp. pure vanilla

Sift together flour, baking powder, xanthan gum, and cream of tartar. In a separate bowl, cream together sugar and butter. Beat for 1–2 minutes. Add egg and vanilla and mix to combine. Add flour mixture and combine. Cover and refrigerate dough for 1 hour. Roll chilled dough between two pieces of wax paper to ½-inch thickness. Cut dough with cookie cutters.

Place on ungreased cookie sheet. Bake at 350 degrees for 8–10 minutes. Cool completely and frost with Vanilla Buttercream Frosting (see page 19).

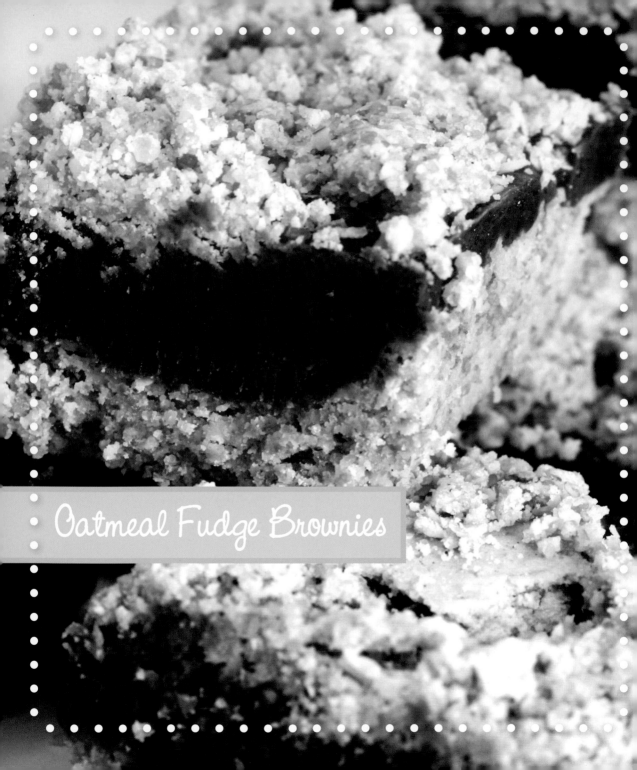

Oatmeal Fudge Brownies

Oatmeal Fudge Brownies

These bars are chewy and yummy. But resist eating them until they are totally cooled. Otherwise, they will end up being a pile of oats and fudge on your plate.

¾ cup butter

1½ cups brown sugar

2 eggs

2 tsp. vanilla

3 cups gluten-free oats, pulsed several times in a food processor to make oats smaller

1 tsp. cinnamon

1½ cups gluten-free flour mix

½ cup buckwheat flour

1 tsp. xanthan gum

1 tsp. baking soda

2 cups gluten-free semi sweet chocolate chips

1 can sweetened condensed milk

½ cup butter

Cream butter, sugar, eggs, and 1 teaspoon vanilla. Slowly add oats, cinnamon, flours, xanthan gum, and baking soda to creamed butter mixture.

Divide dough, and place ⅔ of it on the bottom of a lightly greased 9 × 13 pan. The batter will be thin.

In a saucepan, melt chocolate, condensed milk, butter, and 1 teaspoon vanilla. Pour over bottom layer. Sprinkle remaining crust over the top of the fudge.

Bake at 350 degrees for 25 minutes. Remove from oven and cool completely before cutting into squares.

Beany Blondies

I know what you are thinking. Beans can't be in brownies. Oh, yes they can.
They add rich flavor, healthy protein, and thick texture.

1 (15-oz.) can Garbanzo
    beans, rinsed and drained

½ cup seedless raspberry
    jam (or strawberry)

¼ cup natural crunchy
    peanut butter

¼ cup ground flax seed

2 tsp. vanilla

2 Tbsp. almond flour

¾ tsp. baking powder

Process all ingredients in a food processor until batter is thick and smooth. Lightly grease an 8x8 baking pan. Pour batter inside and make level, spreading batter to all corners.

Bake at 350 degrees for 25–28 minutes. Sprinkle with cinnamon and sugar if desired. Cool and cut into squares.

My Little Monkeys

I swear I gave birth to monkeys the way we eat bananas at our house. Here is a great cookie bar recipe with bananas in case you have several ripe ones left over. Using a bag of gluten-free semi-sweet chocolate chips on top as a frosting is optional, but it is one option I always insist on. Dusting the top with powdered sugar is nice too.

1 Tbsp. vegetable oil

1 cup brown sugar

3 ripe bananas, mashed

2 tsp. vanilla

1 egg

¼ cup buttermilk

2 cups gluten-free flour mix

1 tsp. xanthan gum

1 tsp. cream of tartar

2 tsp. baking powder

2 tsp. cinnamon

pinch of salt

1 bag gluten-free semi-sweet chocolate chip (optional for frosting)

Cream oil and sugar together, adding bananas and vanilla. Add egg and buttermilk and stir to combine all wet ingredients. Add flour, xanthan gum, cream of tartar, baking powder, cinnamon, and a pinch of salt. Stir to moisten all ingredients.

Pour batter into a greased 9x9-inch square pan and bake at 350 degrees for 25–30 minutes or until a toothpick comes out clean. Remove from oven. Sprinkle chocolate chips on hot bars and allow to cool for 2 minutes. Spread melted chips on top of bar. Cool bars completely before cutting into squares. Store in an airtight container.

No-Bake Peanut Butter Fudge

No-Bake Peanut Butter Fudge

This recipe came from an idea behind one of my favorite chocolate peanut butter pies. It's not only easy, but it's fun to make too.

½ cup melted butter

1 cup chopped peanuts

2 cups natural peanut butter

1 pound powdered sugar

gluten-free chocolate, melted (optional)

Place all ingredients in a food processor, and process until thick and creamy texture. Batter will be thick. Spread evenly into a 9×13 lightly greased pan. Chill until firm before you cut into squares.

Drizzle with melted gluten-free chocolate for garnish if desired.

Cranberry Nut Bars

I was thinking of all the great flavors that are savory and thought of this bar.
It will surprise you how easy it is and that it really is a no-bake recipe.

1½ cups blanched almonds

1 cup shredded coconut

6 Tbsp. olive oil

4 Tbsp. raw sugar

1 (16-oz.) frozen cranberries

4 Tbsp. cornstarch (or potato starch)

¾ cup raw sugar

1 tablespoon lemon zest

2 Tbsp. lemon juice

In a food processor, combine almonds and coconut and process until fine. Slowly drizzle in olive oil and sugar to make a crust. Press crust mixture into a greased 9×9 baking dish. Refrigerate 30 minutes to harden.

Meanwhile, in a medium saucepan, place frozen cranberries and toss in the cornstarch or potato starch and remaining sugar. Simmer on medium heat until cranberries are reduced by half and thickened. Add ¾ cup sugar, lemon juice, and lemon zest. Let cool. Pour cranberry mixture on top of chilled crust and refrigerate again for at least 1 hour, or until cranberry mixture is set. Cut into squares.

Surprisingly Vegan

Cookies

Black and White Crisps
Spiced Cranberry Cookies
Magical Macaroons
Autumn Pumpkin Cookies
Lemon Poppy Seed Cookies
No-Bake Peanut Butter Cookies
Olive Oil Peanut Butter Cookies
Gingerbread
Tropical Paradise
Vegan Sugar Cookies

Brownies

Cinnamon Delight
Black Bean Brownies

Bars

Not Your Traditional
   Lemon Squares
Chocolate Peppermint Bars

Argentine Dulce de Leche
   Winner—Best Cookie Contest

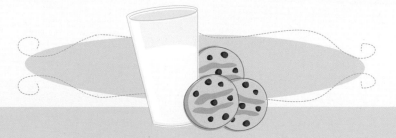

Black and White Crisps

These little black and white cookies are so fantastic and look great on a party or holiday platter.

1 pkg. instant yeast

½ cup soy milk (warm)

½ cup margarine

½ tsp. vanilla

½ tsp. lemon extract

1 cup agave nectar

3 cups flour

½ tsp. salt

Preheat oven to 375 degrees. Add yeast to warm milk and let stand for 5 minutes to proof. Meanwhile, cream together margarine, extracts, and agave nectar. Add dry ingredients to the wet ingredients, and mix until barely combined. Drop by small cookie scoop onto an oiled or sprayed cookie sheet. Press down on cookie with a glass to ½-inch thickness. Bake for 20–25 minutes or until edges of cookie are golden. Remove from oven and cool completely. Frost.

¼ cup vegan semi-sweet chocolate chips

2 Tbsp. cocoa powder

½ tsp. vanilla

¼ tsp. lemon juice

¾ to 1 cup powdered sugar

1 Tbsp. light corn syrup

1 Tbsp. light corn syrup

½ tsp. vanilla

¼ tsp. lemon juice

1¼ cup powdered sugar

Black Frosting: Melt chocolate chips and stir in cocoa. Add rest of ingredients and whisk until all lumps disappear. Frost remaining half of cookie with a butter knife.

White Frosting: Whisk together until no lumps appear. Frost ½ cookie with a butter knife, making a line down the middle.

Spiced Cranberry Cookies

This is one of my favorite textures for an oatmeal cookie, vegan style. It is perfection.

1½ cups whole wheat flour
(or spelt flour)

1 tsp. baking soda

1 tsp. baking powder

½ tsp. kosher salt

¾ cup margarine, softened

1 cup agave nectar
(or raw sugar)

½ cup unsweetened
applesauce

1 tsp. vanilla

1 tsp. cinnamon

½ tsp. nutmeg

½ cup quick oats

½ cup shredded coconut

½ cup dried cranberries

1 cup chopped nuts
(optional)

1 cup vegan chocolate chips

Mix together flour, soda, baking powder, and salt. Set aside.

In a large bowl, beat margarine until light and fluffy. Add agave nectar, applesauce, and vanilla. Add spices and oats, coconut, cranberries, and nuts (optional). Add flour a little at a time, and mix until combined. Fold in chocolate chips. Drop by large cookie scoop onto a greased baking sheet. Bake at 350 degrees for 10–12 minutes.

Magical Macaroons

These macaroons, whether you are vegan or not, will become a favorite. This recipe is easy and fool proof. It takes only a few ingredients to prepare. These cookies also store well in the freezer. But beware, they are really good frozen too.

1¼ cups coconut milk
(light milk is okay too)

2 Tbsp. maple syrup

3 Tbsp. flour

2 cups flaked coconut

½ cup raw sugar
or agave nectar

1 tsp. coconut extract

pinch of sea salt

In a medium saucepan, bring coconut milk, syrup, and flour to a boil, whisking to reduce lumps. Cook 5–7 minutes, stirring frequently until sauce thickens.

Add coconut flakes, sugar, coconut extract, and the salt. Stir to combine. Using a cookie scoop, drop onto a lightly greased cookie sheet.

Bake at 350 degrees for 15 minutes. Dip in chocolate to make these little cookies more decorative.

Autumn Pumpkin Cookies

Autumn Pumpkin Cookies

In our family, if the recipe is great, we call it a keeper. This pumpkin recipe is a keeper, one I will continue to make over and over again.

1 cup canned pumpkin

⅓ cup unsweetened applesauce

1 cup brown sugar (or ½ cup agave nectar)

1 tsp. pumpkin pie spice

3 cups quick oats

1½ cups unbleached flour

1 tsp. baking soda

Mix together pumpkin, applesauce, sugar (or agave), and spice. Combine with dry ingredients and mix until combined.

Bake at 350 degrees for 9–11 minutes or until golden. Remove from oven and cool completely.

Lemon Poppy Seed

Lemon Poppy Seed Cookies

Lemon is truly one of the best flavors around. Poppy seeds aren't too bad either. This dough is so good, I have to suck on a mint to keep myself from eating all of the batter before baking it. But what they say is true—if the cookie dough is great, the cookie will be even better!

¾ cup raw sugar

1 cup margarine

⅓ cup agave nectar
   (or ¾ cup brown sugar)

1 tsp. vanilla

1 tsp. lemon extract

1 cup soy yogurt

1 tsp. baking soda

2 tsp. lemon zest

3 cups unbleached flour

1 tablespoon poppy seeds

Cream together sugar and margarine, adding agave nectar (or brown sugar). Add vanilla, lemon extract, and soy yogurt. Add dry ingredients and poppy seeds, and mix until combined.

Drop by cookie scoop onto oiled baking sheet. Bake at 350 degrees for 9–11 minutes or until lightly golden. Remove from oven and cool completely.

No-Bake Peanut Butter Cookies

No-Bake Peanut Butter Cookies

*Why not? That's right! Something fast and easy that doesn't require baking.
Even I like to have a break from baking now and then.*

1 cup raw sugar

1 cup butter substitute

½ cup soy milk

3 Tbsp. cocoa

½ cup organic peanut butter
(not too oily)

1 tsp. vanilla

3 cups quick oats

½ cup shredded coconut

Boil sugar, margarine, soy milk, and cocoa for 1 minute. Add peanut butter, vanilla, oats, and coconut. Mix well.

Remove from heat and drop onto wax paper by teaspoons. Cool and enjoy.

Olive Oil Peanut Butter Cookies

My sister-in-law loves to cook with various flours other than wheat.
I think she will like this one as much as I do.

½ cup extra virgin olive oil

½ cup agave nectar

1 cup organic peanut butter (chunky can be used; try to get a peanut butter that doesn't have a lot of extra oils)

2 cups whole wheat flour (or spelt flour)

½ tsp. sea salt

1 tsp. baking soda

Mix together olive oil, agave nectar, and peanut butter. Stir until combined. Add dry ingredients and stir until most of the flour disappears. Give one or two more quick stirs. Don't overmix.

Chill for 30 minutes in the refrigerator. Roll into 1-inch balls and place on an oiled cookie sheet. With a fork, make criss-cross marks and bake at 350 degrees for 10 minutes. Remove and cool completely on a wire rack. (If these cookies bake too long, they will become more crumbly.)

Gingerbread

Gingerbread is one of those flavors that bring back the memories of yesterday. A flavor that can transport your mind to another place, to another time, and to another season. Gingerbread makes me feel warm and safe . . . like home.

1 cup dark brown sugar

½ cup molasses

⅓ cup vegetable oil

⅓ cup unsweetened applesauce

1 tsp. vanilla

2–2¼ cups flour

1 tsp. ground ginger

¾ tsp. cinnamon

1 tsp. baking powder

Mix together sugar, molasses, oil, and applesauce until well combined. Add extract and ginger, stirring gently. In a separate bowl, combine flour and spices, stirring until combined. Add half of dry ingredients to wet, stirring just until there is no more white flour showing. Then add the rest. This dough should not be sticky and should form a ball when pressed together in your hand. Add more flour or applesauce, depending on the consistency you have.

Roll dough on a slightly floured surface to ⅓-inch thickness. Cut or shape dough and place on a greased cookie sheet. Bake at 350 degrees for 10–12 minutes. Frost if desired.

Tropical Paradise

Tropical Paradise

*Who doesn't like the flavors of paradise? Coconut, cinnamon, and orange zest
round out these flavors and make this cookie shine. Enjoy every single bite.
Pretend for a moment you are in your very own paradise.*

1 cup unsweetened
   applesauce

¾ cup raw sugar
   (or ¾ cup agave nectar)

2 Tbsp. orange zest

1 Tbsp. ground flax seed

½ cup shredded coconut

1 tsp. coconut extract

3 Tbsp. water

1 cup grated carrots

2 cups unbleached flour

2 tsp. baking powder

1 tsp. cinnamon

pinch of salt

Mix together applesauce, sugar, orange zest, flax seed, shredded coconut, and coconut extract. Add water and carrots.

In a separate bowl, mix together flour, baking powder, cinnamon, and salt. Add dry ingredients to the wet, stirring only until ingredients are combined. Do not overstir.

Drop by tablespoon full onto a lightly greased cookie sheet and bake at 375 degrees for 12–14 minutes or until cookies are golden on the edges. These cookies taste better if not overbaked.

Vegan Sugar Cookies

I can't have a vegan cookie section and not include a great sugar cookie.

1 cup margarine

1 cup sugar

2 whole egg substitutes

1 tsp. vanilla

½ cup soft tofu

3¾–4 cups flour

2 tsp. baking powder

Cream together margarine and sugar until light and fluffy. Add egg substitutes, vanilla, and tofu. Mix to combine. Add flour and baking powder, and mix until dough comes together. Cover and refrigerate for at least 1 hour. Roll chilled dough between 2 pieces of wax paper to ½-inch thickness. Cut dough with cookie cutter and place on parchment lined cookie sheet. Bake at 350 degrees for 12–15 minutes or until slightly golden. Remove from oven and cool completely before frosting.

Note: You can frost with Vanilla Buttercream Frosting (see page 19) by changing ingredients to equal parts margarine and soy milk.

Cinnamon Delight

These brownies have a great flavor, are easy to make, and are chewy and delicious. I made them for my family, and sadly enough, we ate the whole dish in one sitting.

½ cup raw sugar

1¼ cup unsweetened applesauce

1¼ tsp. vanilla

⅓ cup cocoa powder

¾ cup unbleached white flour

2 tsp. baking powder

½ tsp. soda

dash of cinnamon

½ cup semi-sweet vegan chocolate chips

Mix together sugar, applesauce, vanilla, and cocoa powder. Gently add dry ingredients to the wet, folding in vegan chocolate chips.

Pour into a lightly sprayed or oiled 8×8 baking dish. Bake at 350 degrees for 25–30 minutes. Remove and cool completely. Cut into squares.

Black Bean Brownies

Black Bean Brownies

These brownies are dense because they don't have flour. They are packed with protein and are a healthier version. No one will know they have beans in them!

2 ripe bananas, mashed

⅓ cup agave nectar
   (or ⅔ cup raw sugar)

⅔ cup unsweetened
   applesauce

1 (15-oz.) can black beans,
   rinsed and drained

¼ cup cocoa

½ cup whole wheat flour

1 tsp. vanilla

1 Tbsp. cinnamon (optional)

½ cup quick oats

Mix together all ingredients, except oats, in a food processor. Process batter until thick and smooth. Add oats and process again until combined.

Pour into oiled 8×8 pan and bake at 350 degrees for 30 minutes. Brownie will be really fudgy. Cool completely and cut into squares. (If you want a more cake-like brownie, you can add ¼ cup more quick oats or ¼ cup unbleached flour.) This recipe does not freeze well. Dust with powdered sugar if desired.

Not Your Traditional Lemon Squares

For anyone who hasn't tried tofu, this recipe is a great one. This recipe was inspired by my best Luscious Lemon Bar. Lemony goodness in the form of a square. Pure delight!

½ cup margarine, softened

2 Tbsp. lemon zest, divided

½ cup powdered sugar

1 cup plus 3 Tbsp. flour, divided

½ cup silken tofu (soft)

⅓ cup lemon juice

1 Tbsp. cornstarch

1 cup sugar

¼ cup powdered sugar

Combine margarine, 1 tablespoon lemon zest, ½ cup powdered sugar, and 1 cup flour in a food processor. Process until mixture becomes a crumb texture. Press crumbs into a greased 8×8 baking dish, spreading evenly to form a crust.

Bake at 350 degrees for 15 minutes. In a food processor, or by hand (this takes more muscle strength), combine tofu, lemon juice, cornstarch, sugar, and remaining lemon zest. Pour over baked crust and bake for 25 more minutes. Remove from oven and cool. Dust with powdered sugar and cut into squares.

Chocolate Peppermint Bars

Winter is the season for treats such as this, but why wait to make this special cookie bar? To make the frosting red, add red food coloring instead of green. Or to make your presentation beautiful, do a batch of each color. I love the three layers of this cookie!

1¼ cup vegan semi-sweet chocolate chips

½ cup soy milk

⅓ cup margarine

1 cup sugar (or ½ cup agave nectar)

1 tsp. vanilla

⅔ cup cocoa powder

2 cups flour

Melt chocolate chips in a glass bowl, stirring often. Add soy milk, margarine, and sugar (or agave) to the chocolate, and stir to combine. Then add vanilla and cocoa. Add flour and stir until combined. Oil and layer an 8×8 baking dish with parchment paper (this is important!). Spread dough evenly on parchment paper and bake at 350 degrees for 15–18 minutes. Remove from oven and cool completely.

½ cup margarine

2 Tbsp. or more soy milk

2 tsp. peppermint extract

2½ cups powdered sugar

3–4 drops green food coloring

Filling: Beat margarine until light. Add milk, extract, and powdered sugar. It will resemble a thick frosting texture. Add food coloring and blend well. Layer evenly on cooled crust.

1½ cups vegan semi-sweet chocolate chips

2 Tbsp. vegetable shortening

Topping: Melt chocolate chips and shortening together and stir to combine. Pour onto peppermint frosting and spread to make an even layer. Place in refrigerator to cool completely. This cookie is easier to cut into squares when chilled.

Argentine dulce de leche

BY JULIANA ALONSO DOROLA

I love traveling, painting, photography, baking, and drawing. I'm a graphic designer and a pastry chef. I would love to mix all the things I love and make them my job. I'm also trying to start a small catering business for children's parties. To see more of my baking adventures visit, http://horneandoalogo.blogspot.com
Thank you, Juliana, and congratulations!

¾ cup butter

¾ cup sugar

3 egg yolks

2 Tbsp. dark rum or rum extract

1½ cups flour

1 cup plus 1 Tbsp. cornstarch

1 Tbsp. instant yeast

dulce de leche for filling

Beat butter and sugar until smooth and creamy. Add egg yolks, beating one at a time, until completely incorporated. Add rum and mix until combined. Sift dry ingredients together and add to wet mixture. Combine well and refrigerate for at least 2 hours. Roll out chilled dough on a floured surface to ⅛–¼-inch thickness. Cut into small circles with a cookie cutter.

Place cookies on a lightly greased cookie sheet. Bake at 350 degrees for 8 minutes or until the edges are slightly golden. Remove from oven and cool completely. Spread dulce de leche filling in the middle of one cookie and top with another cookie. Drizzle with caramel sauce or dust with powdered sugar.

Index

Ginger Chocolate Snaps, 105

Gingerbread, 127

Grandma Lu's Persimmon Cookies, 27

Grandma Y's German Cookies, 13

Harvest Pumpkin Cookies, 101

Julia's Molasses Cookies, 36

Lemon Drop Cookies, 103

Lemon Poppy Seed Cookies, 123

Magical Macaroons, 119

Make Some Whoopie Pies, 25

Mini Peanut Butter Bites, 31

No-Bake Peanut Butter Cookies, 125

Oatmeal Butterscotch Cookies, 35

Olive Oil Peanut Butter Cookies, 126

Olive Oil Shortbread, 94

Peanut Butter Bliss, 102

Peanut Butter Goodness, 9

Piña Colada Cookies
  with a Coconut Glaze, 23

Pumpkin Chocolate Cookies, 90

Root beer Float Cookies
  with a Cream Glaze, 21

Rosemary & Lavender Shortbread
  with a Lavender Glaze, 15

Simply Peanut Butter Cookies, 85

Soft Sour Cream Sugar Cookies
  with a Vanilla Buttercream Frosting, 19

Spectacular Snickerdoodles, 7

Spiced Cranberry Cookies, 118

Spicy Applesauce Oatmeal Cookies, 86

Sunny Lemonade Cookies, 37

Tropical Paradise, 128

Vegan Sugar Cookies, 130

White Chocolate Gems, 12

Whole Wheat Sugar Cookies, 87

Cowboy Up, 39

Cranberry Nut Bars, 114

Crazy for Cranberries
  *with a Cream Cheese Frosting
  and White Chocolate Drizzle*, 51

Creamy Lemon Blueberry Delight, 43

O

Oatmeal Butterscotch Cookies, 35

Oatmeal Fudge Brownies, 109

Olive Oil Peanut Butter Cookies, 126

Olive Oil Shortbread, 94

P

Peanut Butter Bliss, 102

Peanut Butter Cup Brownies, 69

Peanut Butter Goodness, 9

Perfectly Peanut Butter Bars, 57

Piña Colada Cookies
  with a Coconut Glaze, 23

Pumpkin Chocolate Cookies, 90

R

Root beer Float Cookies
  with a Cream Glaze, 21

Rosemary & Lavender Shortbread
  with a Lavender Glaze, 15

S

Simply Peanut Butter Cookies, 85

Sinful Chocolate Raspberry Brownies
  with a Raspberry Glaze, 71

Soft Sour Cream Sugar Cookies
  with a Vanilla Buttercream Frosting, 19

Southern Sweet Potato Bars
  with Maple Glaze, 53

Spectacular Snickerdoodles, 7

Spiced Cranberry Cookies, 118

Spicy Applesauce Oatmeal Cookies, 86

Sunny Lemonade Cookies, 37

Surprise, Surprise! Brownies, 96

T

There's Zucchini in here?, 79

Traditional Nanaimo Bars, 61

Triple Chocolate Fudge Brownies, 63

Tropical Paradise, 129

V

Vegan Sugar Cookies, 130

W

White Chocolate Gems, 12

White Chocolate Macadamia Blondies, 66

Whole Wheat Sugar Cookies, 87

About the Author

Wendy L. Paul has been cooking and baking for many years. She enjoys writing new recipes and creating easy-to-make dinners and desserts. When Wendy is working on a project—whether home improvement, a new recipe, or shopping at a craft store—she is truly happy. She previously authored *101 Gourmet Cupcakes in 10 Minutes*. She and her family live in Utah, and oddly enough have a dog named Cupcake. For more information, visit her website at *www.wendypaulcreations.com*.

About the Photographer

Marielle Hayes is a photographer based in the San Francisco Bay Area. When she is not behind the camera, she enjoys traveling and spending time with her friends and family. She resides in Oakland Hills with her husband, daughter, and Boston Terrier.